ANCIENT MARINE LIFE

SEA SCORPIONS

BY KATE MOENING
ILLUSTRATIONS BY MAT EDWARDS

EPIC

BELLWETHER MEDIA • MINNEAPOLIS, MN

EPIC

EPIC BOOKS are no ordinary books. They burst with intense action, high-speed heroics, and shadows of the unknown. Are you ready for an Epic adventure?

This edition first published in 2023 by Bellwether Media, Inc.

No part of this publication may be reproduced in whole or in part without written permission of the publisher. For information regarding permission, write to Bellwether Media, Inc., Attention: Permissions Department, 6012 Blue Circle Drive, Minnetonka, MN 55343.

Library of Congress Cataloging-in-Publication Data

LC record for Sea Scorpions available at: https://lccn.loc.gov/2022050385

Text copyright © 2023 by Bellwether Media, Inc. EPIC and associated logos are trademarks and/or registered trademarks of Bellwether Media, Inc.

Editor: Betsy Rathburn   Designer: Jeffrey Kollock

Printed in the United States of America, North Mankato, MN.

TABLE OF CONTENTS

WHAT WERE SEA SCORPIONS?

Sea scorpions were the biggest **arthropods** to ever exist! They lived during the **Paleozoic era.** They were most common in the **Silurian period.**

MAP OF THE WORLD

Silurian period

Most sea scorpions were less than 2 feet (0.6 meters) long. The biggest grew over 8 feet (2.4 meters) long!

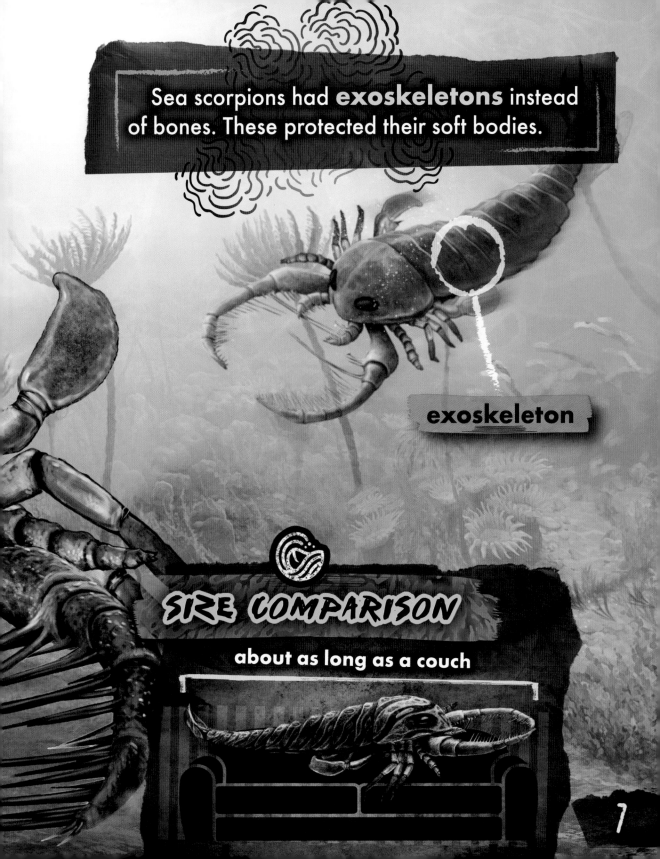

Sea scorpions had **exoskeletons** instead of bones. These protected their soft bodies.

exoskeleton

SIZE COMPARISON

about as long as a couch

Sea scorpions had six pairs of legs.
Many had paddle-shaped back legs.
These helped them swim.

They used their front legs to rip apart **prey**. They used their middle legs to walk!

paddle-shaped back leg

prey

THE LIVES OF SEA SCORPIONS

Early sea scorpions lived in ocean waters. Over time, most moved into **freshwater.**

Some sea scorpions swam through deep waters in search of prey. Others did not swim much. They walked along river bottoms instead.

FIELD TRIP

Most sea scorpions spent their lives underwater. But some could go on land for short periods of time.

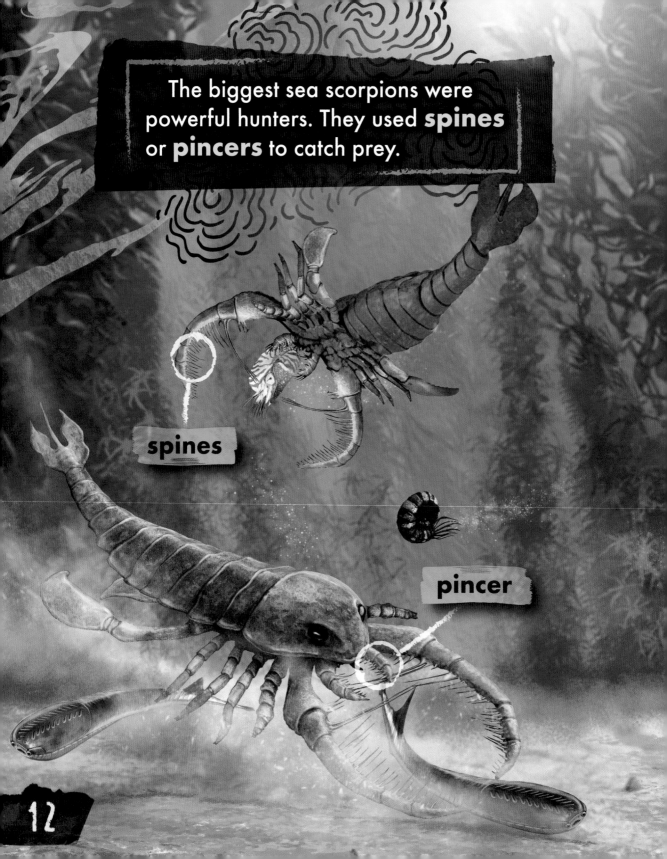

The biggest sea scorpions were powerful hunters. They used **spines** or **pincers** to catch prey.

spines

pincer

Sea scorpions mostly ate fish and **mollusks**. They also ate other sea scorpions!

SEA SCORPION DIET

fish

mollusks

sea scorpions

Sea scorpions mostly lived alone. But they may have gathered in **shallow** areas to lay eggs.

Babies stayed in these shallow waters until they got bigger. Then they moved into deeper water.

FOSSILS AND EXTINCTION

ALL IN THE FAMILY

There were more than 200 kinds of sea scorpions! Today's scorpions and spiders are related to them.

About 250 million years ago, Earth's oceans warmed. Almost all life on Earth went **extinct** during this time. Sea scorpions could not survive the changes. They died out, too.

FOSSIL FINDS

Sea scorpions shed their exoskeletons as they grew. Many fossils are actually outgrown exoskeletons!

fossils

The first sea scorpion **fossil** was found in New York in 1818. A large ocean once covered this area.

BIGGEST COMPLETE SEA SCORPION FOSSIL

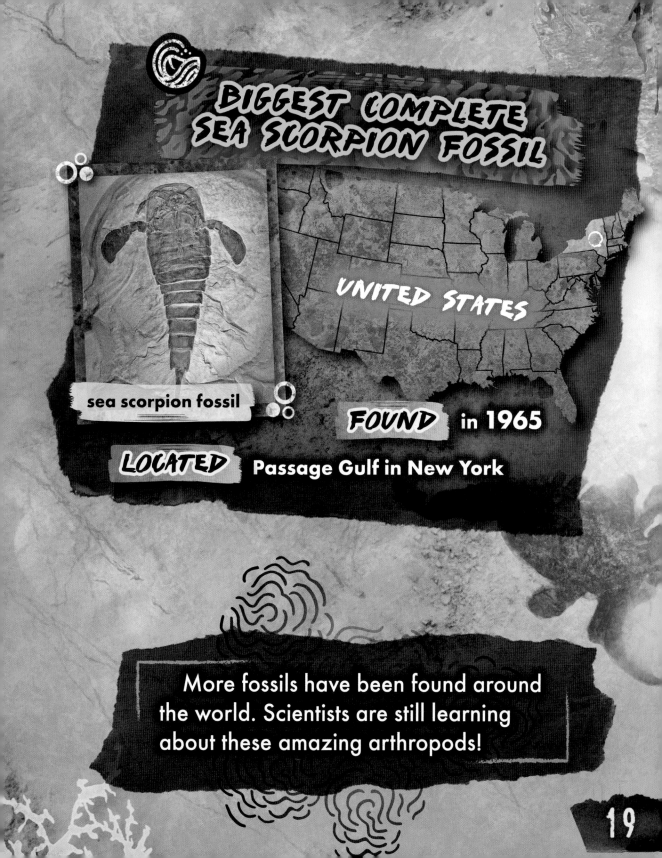

sea scorpion fossil

UNITED STATES

FOUND in 1965

LOCATED Passage Gulf in New York

More fossils have been found around the world. Scientists are still learning about these amazing arthropods!

GET TO KNOW THE SEA SCORPION

paddle-shaped back legs

LOCATION
around the world, mostly in Europe and North America

FOOD
fish

mollusks

sea scorpions

SIZE
over 8 feet (2.4 meters) long

exoskeleton

spines

FIRST FOSSIL FOUND

in 1818 by S.L. Mitchill

GLOSSARY

arthropods—animals with segmented bodies and no backbone; most arthropods have exoskeletons that they shed from time to time.

exoskeletons—hard outer coverings of arthropods; exoskeletons protect and support arthropod bodies.

extinct—no longer living

fossil—the remains of a living thing that lived long ago

freshwater—water that is not salty; lakes, rivers, and streams are all freshwater environments.

mollusks—animals that have soft bodies and usually have a hard outer shell; some mollusks, such as squids, have an inner shell.

Paleozoic era—a time in history that happened about 541 million to 252 million years ago; many new kinds of ocean life appeared during the Paleozoic era.

pincers—body parts used to grab food

prey—animals that are hunted by other animals for food

shallow—not deep

Silurian period—the third period of the Paleozoic era that occurred between 443 million and 419 million years ago

spines—sharp, pointed body parts of some sea scorpions

TO LEARN MORE

AT THE LIBRARY

Amin, Anita Nahta. *Dig and Discover Fossils*. North Mankato, Minn.: Capstone Press, 2023.

Rake, Matthew. *Prehistoric Sea Beasts*. Minneapolis, Minn.: Hungry Tomato, 2017.

Taylor, Charlotte. *Digging Up Sea Creature Fossils*. New York, N.Y.: Enslow Publishing, 2022.

ON THE WEB

FACTSURFER

Factsurfer.com gives you a safe, fun way to find more information.

1. Go to www.factsurfer.com.

2. Enter "sea scorpions" into the search box and click 🔍 .

3. Select your book cover to see a list of related content.

INDEX

The images in this book are reproduced through the courtesy of: Mat Edwards, front cover, pp. 1, 2, 3, 4-5, 6-7, 8-9, 10-11, 12-13, 14-15, 16-17, 18-19, 20-21; H. Zell/ Wikipedia, p. 19 (fossil); Gdr/ Wikipedia, p. 21 (S.L. Mitchill).